Spokane

impressions

FARCOUNTRY
PRESS

Front cover: River Park Square, downtown Spokane.

Back cover: The grand Davenport Hotel in downtown Spokane.

Right: Work stops in winter on the Palouse, and all is still and silent.

Title page: Convenient lodging, fine dining, and upscale shopping are synonymous with downtown Spokane. Many of the city's downtown blocks are connected by climate-controlled walkways and skywalks.

ISBN: 1-56037-315-6
Photographs © 2004 by Charles Gurche
© 2004 Farcountry Press

For more information on our books write: Farcountry Press, P.O. Box 5630, Helena, MT 59604; call (800) 821-3874; or visit www.farcountrypress.com

Created, produced, and designed in the United States.
Printed in China.

Above: Built in 1914, the Davenport Hotel closed in 1985 but was reopened in 2002 after extensive renovations.

Right: The hotel's lobby glitters again with the refined opulence that made it famous.

Above: A coat of snow adds to the elegance of a stately home in Hutton neighborhood.

Facing page: The Spokane Opera House windows distort downtown's familiar landmark, the Clock Tower, all that remains today of the Great Northern Railway's Spokane station.

Above: Fall scatters hawthorn leaves amid dainty aubrieta growing in Spokane County.

Left: Bikers wheel through a quiet section of Manito Park during a race.

Left: Those who wander down to the banks of the Little Spokane River on a winter morning are not disappointed by the mystical view.

Below: Tranquility reigns in the Japanese Garden of Manito Park. This garden is a symbol of the friendship between Spokane and her sister city in Japan, Nishinomiya.

Right: A solitary Ponderosa pine endures yet another long winter.

Below: The Milk Bottle, built in 1935, is one of Garland Park's better-known landmarks. The fanciful building was constructed for Paul E. Newport's creamery business.

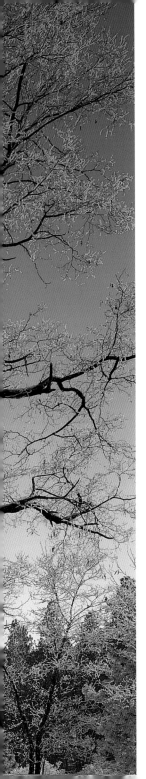

Left: A brittle layer of frost on black locust trees creates a winter wonderland.

Below: Water rushes over the basalt formations of the Spokane River's lower falls.

Facing page: A fine example of Neo-Classical Revival architecture, the Masonic Temple was completed in 1905. It represents the significance of the fraternal and social organizations that met within its halls for many years.

Below: A pensive lion gazes at visitors in Cat Tales Zoological Park, a favorite destination of old and young alike. Cat Tales also offers a zookeeping program, which attracts students from all over the country.

Left: Wildflowers abound in Turnbull National Wildlife Refuge. Nearly 16,000 acres provide a sanctuary for ducks, geese, and other migratory birds as well as many types of mammals.

Below: Students and Spokane residents worship at Saint Aloysius Church on the Gonzaga University campus. Founded initially as a boy's boarding school in 1887, the university was named for the Jesuit Saint Aloysius Gonzaga, the patron of youth.

Left: The Spokane County Courthouse would be right at home in the Loire Valley of France. Its towers and turrets, iron and brickwork are reminiscent of a French Renaissance chateau.

Facing page: The Spokane River attracted settlers who erected a trading post in the area in 1810. However, the turbulent war of 1812 caused the small settlement to be abandoned and it was not permanently resettled until 1871.

Above: Palouse County was given its name, from the French "grassland," for its springtime hills of wheat.

Left: Agriculture has long played a significant role in the regional economy, as these lush fields in Whitman County show.

Above: The hustle and bustle of the city begins to diminish with the arrival of dusk.

Right: A field of lupine, one of Washington's signature wildflowers, blooms at Steptoe Butte State Park. On a clear day, one can see 200 miles from the top of the butte.

Above: Flowerfield, an estate on the Little Spokane River that was built by the Davenports as their retreat from the city, now houses Saint George's School, a private college preparatory school.

Facing page: The brightly painted steeds of the 1909 Looff Carousel at Riverfront Park allure many an eager young rider.

The manicured grounds of Duncan Garden in Manito Park are a memorable setting for summer weddings and other outdoor events.

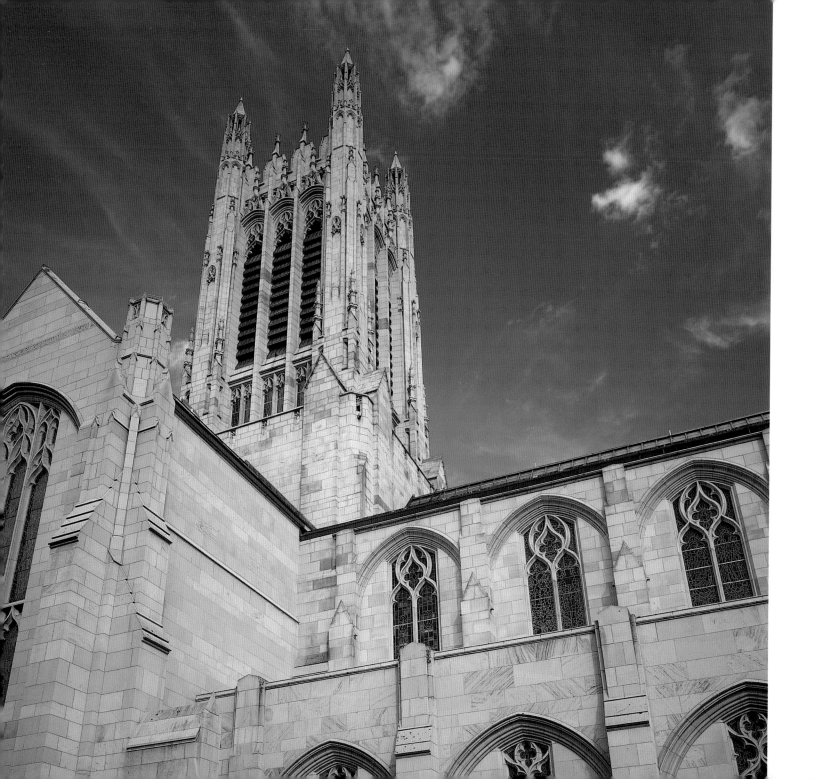

Above & Facing page: Detailed stonework embellishes the magnificent bell tower of St. John's Cathedral. Designed by a congregation member and begun in 1925, the church suggests the English Gothic style but also shows French influence in its construction.

Facing page: The Monroe Street Bridge across the Spokane River Gorge contained the largest concrete central span in the United States when it was completed in 1911.

Below: Gonzaga awarded Bing Crosby, one of Spokane's most famous sons, an honorary doctorate in 1937. This statue sits outside the Crosby Student Center, which houses an impressive collection of the crooner's memorabilia.

Above: The charming facade of the Carnegie Library's Heath Branch, named for Sylvester Heath, one of the founders of Spokane.

Left: Now Waverly Place Bed and Breakfast, this gracious Queen Anne Victorian was constructed in 1902 by Harry J. Skinner, a prominent builder.

Above: Residents of Spokane and surrounding areas enjoy the Centennial Trail, a paved path running from the Idaho state line to Nine Mile Falls, a total of 37 miles within Washington's borders.

Right: Lilacs in full bloom attract residents and visitors to Manito Park.

The Bloomsday Race, one of Spokane's most beloved springtime events, is held the first weekend of May and attracts as many as 60,000 participants.

Above: The glow of Christmas lights on a snowy evening invites passersby to slow down and enjoy the magic of the season.

Facing page: From figure skating to pro basketball to rock concerts, the Spokane Arena hosts an event for everyone.

Above: Both historic and modern bridges span the Spokane River.

Right: This attractive brick structure is one of a number of historic buildings that house the Mukogawa Fort Wright Institute, a branch of Japan's Mukogawa Women's University. Students here immerse themselves in the English language and American culture.

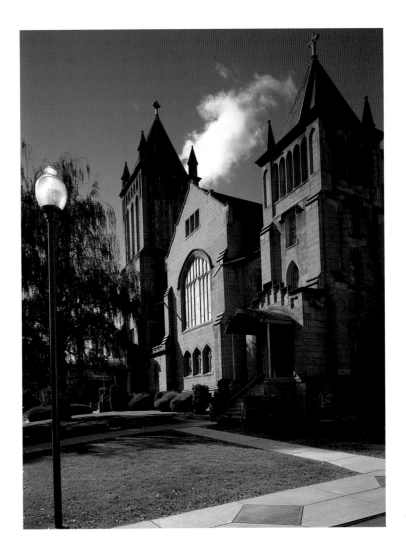

Above: The parishioners of the First Presbyterian Church are always pleased to hear the sweet songs of the children's choir.

Left: Endless stretches of green links entice players to the Indian Canyon Golf Course.

Right: The productive wheat fields of Palouse yield their bounty.

Below: A whimsical sculpture of the Bloomsday Race runners by artist
David Govedare is a major Riverfront Park attraction.

Right: Snow-covered fir trees glow at sunset in Mt. Spokane State Park, which receives up to 300 inches of snow a year.

Below: Spokane's educational options include Eastern Washington University, situated in Cheney, southwest of Spokane.

Above: The 43,000-square-foot Jundt Art Center and Museum at Gonzaga
University is proof of the community's steady support of the arts.

Facing page: In addition to its normal traffic, the Sunset Highway
Bridge occasionally plays host to nesting peregrine falcons.

Facing page: An entrancing study of red maple leaves delights those meandering through the John A. Finch Arboretum. This arboretum features deciduous and evergreen trees from all over the world, as well as many exotic plants.

Below: The Spokane Flour Mill, built in 1895, is now home to many fine restaurants and shops.

Above: Riverside State Park's 10,000 acres of bucolic countryside offer many places to view the rushing Spokane River.

Facing page: Established in 1895, Our Lady of Lourdes Cathedral still houses a faithful community of worshippers.

Left: The gazebo at Coeur d'Alene Park invites visitors to relax. Spokane's first public park is the site of a summer music festival.

Facing page: A rustic stone arch at Riblet Mansion—now home to Arbor Crest Winery—frames the garden beyond.

A restaurant grease fire in August 1889 destroyed
32 blocks of Spokane Falls, including the original
Howard Street Bridge. Now rebuilt, the bridge
faces Riverfront Park.

Right: A lone cottonwood stands in the colorful canola fields of Whitman County.

Below: Spokane residents choose from an array of vegetables and other treats at the local Farmer's Market.

Right and Facing page: Marilyn Monroe and classic cars make an unforgettable impression on visitors to the eclectic Carr's Museum.

Above: The Spokesman-Review, Spokane's only daily newspaper, keeps citizens informed.

Left: The wheat fields of the Palouse ripen for harvest.

Facing page: Snow-covered conifers in Mt. Spokane State Park delight cross-country skiers and other winter visitors to the park.

Below: An elegant swan enjoys the calm waters in Manito Park.

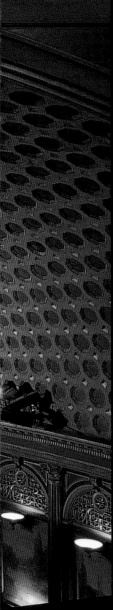

Above: An early freeze encases
hawthorn berries and leaves in ice.

Left: The curtain is ready to rise on another entertaining
theatrical or musical event at the Met Theater.

Above: Students find a peaceful place to work in the recesses of
Whitworth College's library, located on the north side of Spokane.

Right: Expansive meadows in bloom are a delight to travelers venturing to Nine Mile Falls.

Facing page: The Northwest Museum of Arts & Culture was founded in 1918 as the Eastern Washington State Historical Society. After a large donation of Native American artifacts and books, the newly expanded museum opened its doors in 2001.

Left: Canoeing on the Spokane River makes for a refreshing afternoon.

Above: The ultimate in red wagons, Ken Spiering's "Childhood Express" is irresistible to the children of Spokane, to whom this sculpture was given during Washington State's 1989 Centennial.

Right: Sunset paints a lovely scene on Coyote Lake.

Facing page: Although Spokane's population is close to 200,000, its downtown has the feeling of a smaller, more intimate town.

Below: Autumn lays down a golden mantle of leaves in Comstock Park.

Above: A day of climbing at Minnehaha Rock always provides a challenge. These granite outcroppings test both novice and advanced climbers.

Right: Storm clouds gather over Granite Lake, a popular resort just inside the border of Washington.

Charles Gurche is one of the United States' foremost nature and landscape photographers. His work has appeared in numerous calendars and magazines, including *Audubon, National Geographic, Natural History,* and *Outside,* and in the books *Kansas Simply Beautiful, Missouri Simply Beautiful, Oregon Impressions, Virginia Impressions, Virginia Simply Beautiful,* and *Washington Wild and Beautiful.* He has photographed for Kodak, the Sierra Club, Smithsonian Books, and the National Park Service. Gurche has won awards from Roger Tory Peterson Institute and the Society of Professional Journalists.